REGULAR SHOW™

HEY BRO, DID YA KNOW?

BY ERIC LUPER

PSS!
PRICE STERN SLOAN

An Imprint of Penguin Group (USA) LLC

PRICE STERN SLOAN
Published by the Penguin Group
Penguin Group (USA) LLC, 375 Hudson Street, New York, New York 10014, USA

USA | Canada | UK | Ireland | Australia | New Zealand | India | South Africa | China

penguin.com
A Penguin Random House Company

Published in 2015 by Price Stern Sloan, a division of Penguin Young Readers Group, 345 Hudson Street, New York, New York 10014. PSS! is a registered trademark of Penguin Group (USA) LLC. Manufactured in China.

ISBN 978-0-8431-8269-9   10 9 8 7 6 5 4 3 2 1

SKIPS DOES NOT GET ALONG WITH COMPUTERS.

NEVER PASS OUT

RIGBY WAS HERE

WHEN THERE ARE MARKERS ABOUT!

In the Middle Ages, members of the nobility would eat boiled sugar on a stick.

OH THE HUMANITY!!

IT WOULD NOT BE CALLED A LOLLIPOP UNTIL 1908.

WE WILL ERASE YOU FROM EXISTENCE!
NEVER MESS WITH THE MESSENGER!

Drinking ice-cold water can help you lose weight, because it takes energy to raise the temperature of the water to your **BODY TEMPERATURE.**

THE INTERGALACTIC DODGEBALL COUNCIL

DECIDES ALL THINGS DODGE-RELATED.

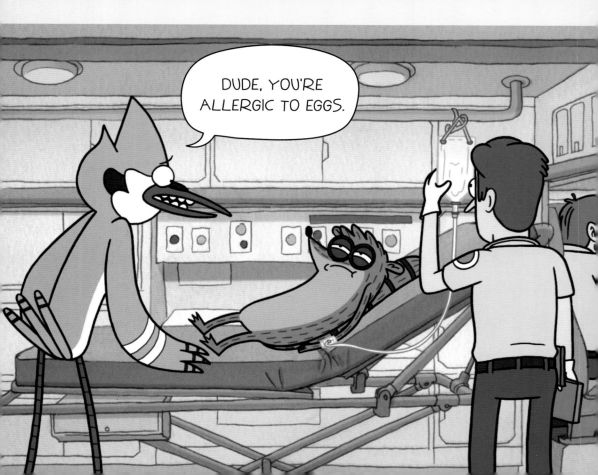

C.J. AND THE THUNDER GIRLS ARE
DODGEBALL CHAMPIONS

The legend of the yeti originated in Tibet. The legend makes no mention of a yeti's skipping skills.

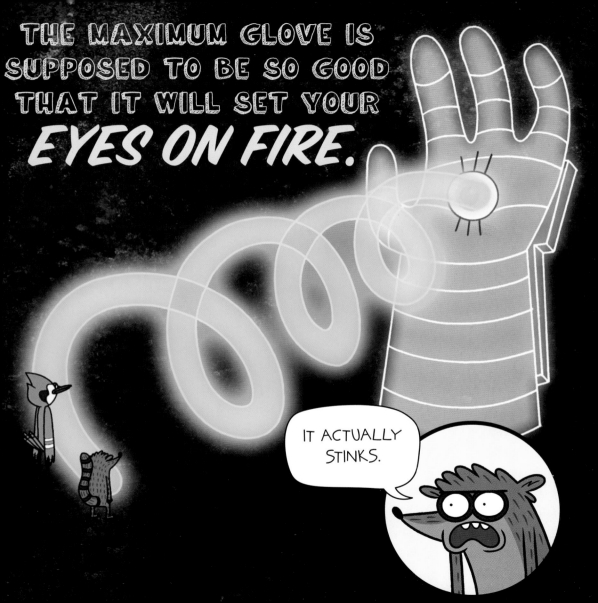

CHILLING IN THE POOL!

MORDECAI & C.J. HAVE BEEN DODGING THE ISSUE.

WHEN MORDECAI AND RIGBY WERE YOUNG, THEY ASKED SANTA CLAUS FOR INVISIBILITY CLOAKS EVERY YEAR.

BUT IT IS AGAINST THE RULES FOR SANTA to give magical gifts.

FANNY PACKS ARE ALSO CALLED BELT PACKS, BELLY BAGS, CHAOS POUCHES, BUFFALO POUCHES, AND BUM BAGS.

ONLY MUSCLE MAN HAS A GRAVY POUCH, THOUGH!

LIST OF PHOBIAS YOU MAY NOT WANT IF YOU WORK AT A PARK:

1. Agrizoophobia: FEAR OF WILD ANIMALS
2. Atychiphobia: FEAR OF FAILURE
3. Ornithophobia: FEAR OF BIRDS
4. Spectrophobia: FEAR OF GHOSTS
5. Xylophobia: FEAR OF TREES AND FORESTS
6. Ephebiphobia: FEAR OF YOUTH

THESE BABY DUCKS HAVE THE COOLEST APARTMENT.
HOW COME WE LIVE IN SUCH A LAME HOUSE?

RIGBY RUNS ON ALL FOURS BUT WALKS ON HIS HIND LEGS.

THE PROPER WAY TO EAT A SANDWICH OF DEATH IS WEARING CUTOFF JEANS AND A MULLET.

WHY WOULD YOU BUY SOMETHING THAT KILLS PEOPLE?

THE FIRST MOTORIZED LAWN MOWERS WERE POWERED BY STEAM ENGINES AND WERE OVER SIX FEET TALL. THEY TOOK SEVERAL HOURS TO WARM UP.

MORDECAI AND RIGBY HAVE BEEN FRIENDS SINCE THEY WERE SIX.
NOW THEY ARE TWENTY-THREE.

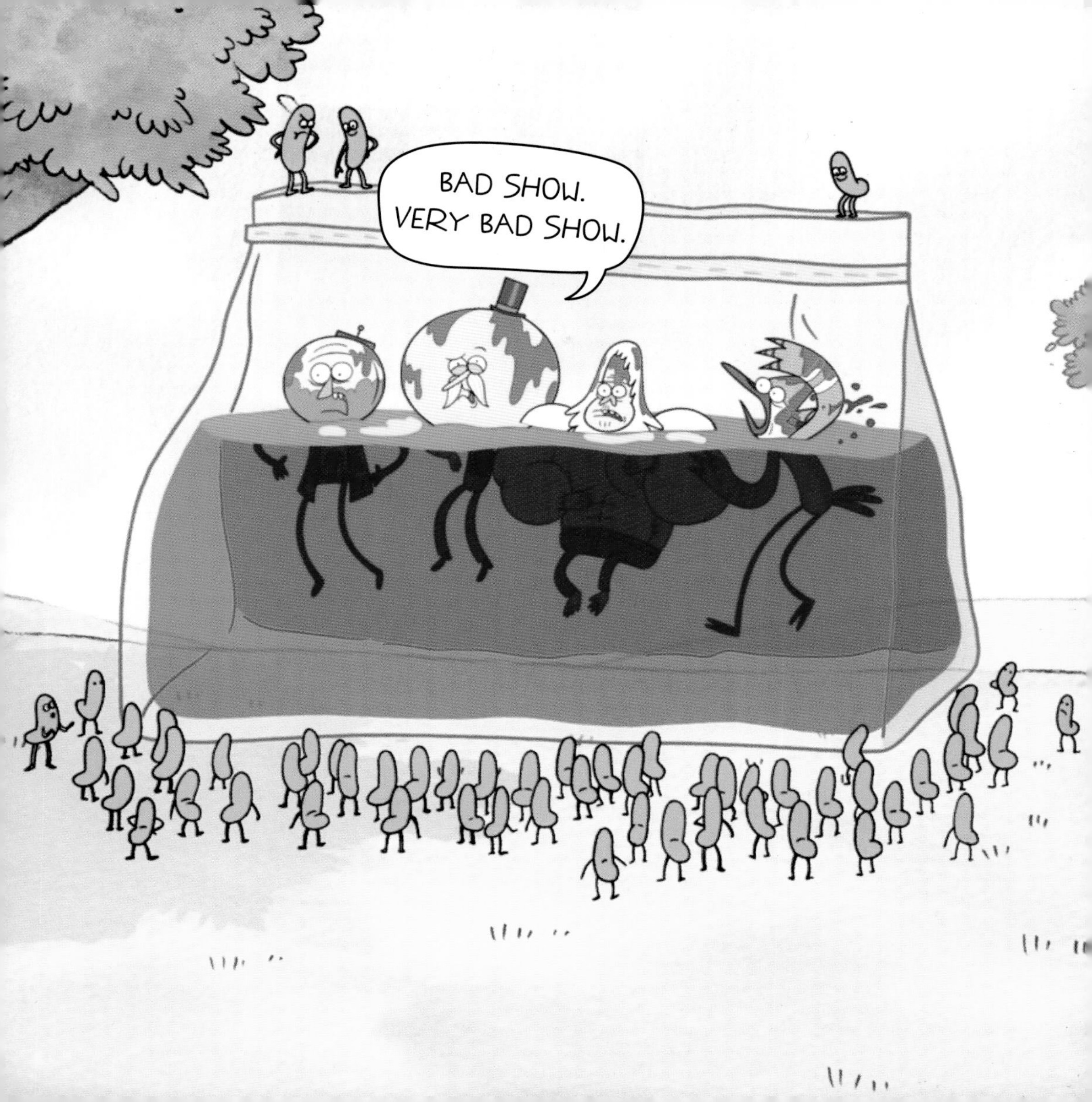
BAD SHOW.
VERY BAD SHOW.

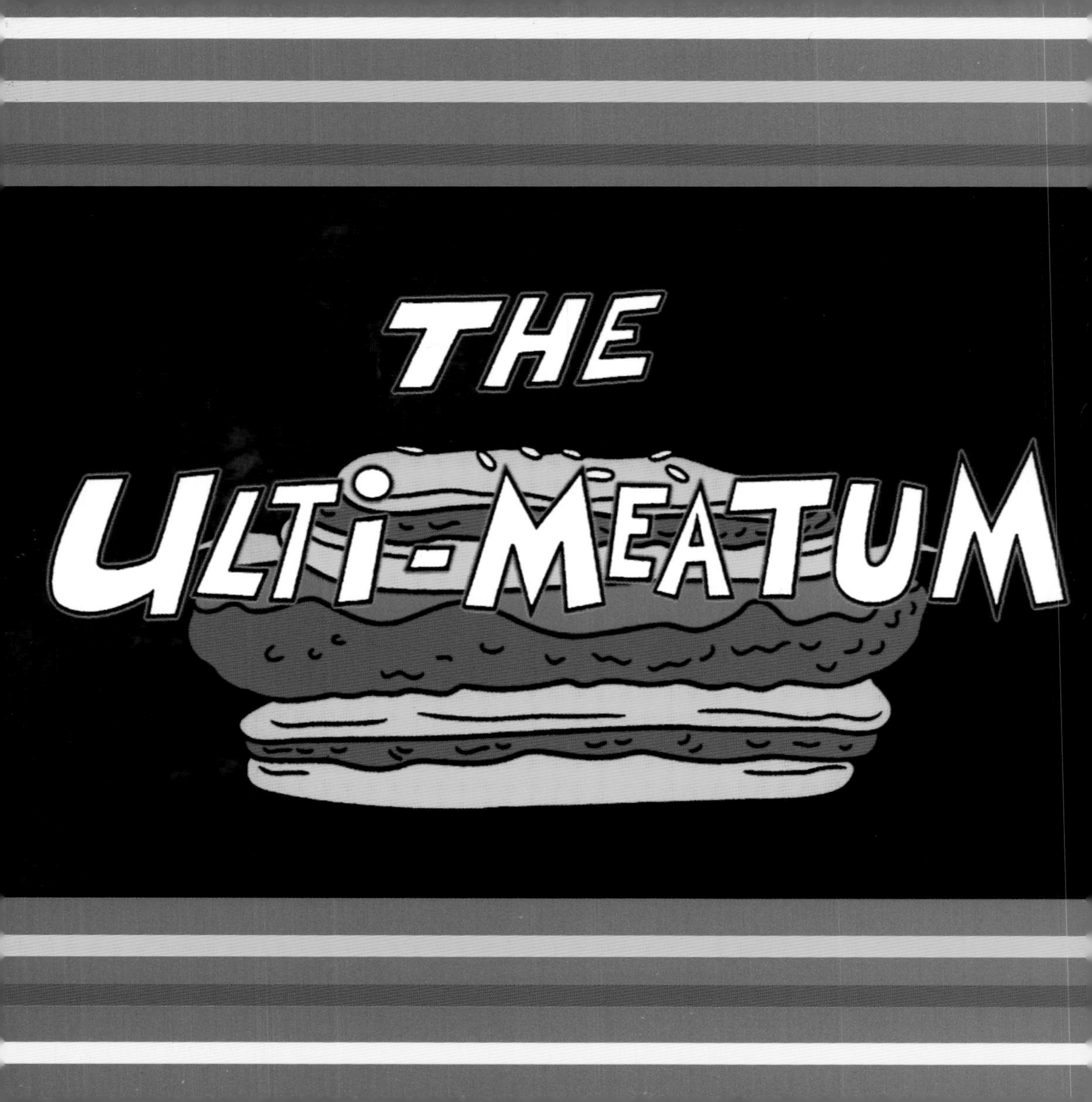
THE
ULTI-MEATUM

MORDECAI'S NICKNAMES:
MORDO
MORDECRY
WRONGECAI
BRODECAI
BLONDECAI
MORDY

CAN'T A GHOST JUST PASS THROUGH CHAINS?

THE MOST FIREWORK ROCKETS SET OFF
IN THIRTY SECONDS IS 125,801.

ROCK-PAPER-SCISSORS IS ALSO KNOWN AS **ROSHAMBO,** PAPER-SCISSORS-STONE, AND ICK-ACK-OCK.

RECIPE FOR AN EGGSCELLENT OMELET:

12 eggs, chili, cheese, biscuits, fruit bowl

THE ART OF TRIMMING BUSHES TO LOOK LIKE ANIMALS IS CALLED TOPIARY.

Although she is supposed to be a robin, Margaret has the markings of a male cardinal.

HACKY SACK IS ALSO CALLED KEEPIE UPPIE. SOME COMMON TRICKS INCLUDE: STALLS, DAGGERS, LIFTS, AND LOOPS.

A CRAZY HARD TRICK IS CALLED PARADOX ILLUSION.

When Margaret is away,
Mordecai is sad.

DEPRESSED MORDECAI IS A CHUMP.

23-YEAR-OLD SBR
(SINGLE BROWN RACCOON)

Likes eating doughnuts, cake, and hamburgers from the trash. Prefers BLTs with no lettuce, no tomatoes, no bread, and double bacon. Favorite cereal is Sugar Frosted Marshmallow Clusters. Hates kittens and taking showers. In search of SBM (single beige mole), preferably without glasses.

STARLA IS EVERYWHERE!

PUTTING TOO MUCH STUFF INTO A DEEP FRYER CREATES A FRY MONSTER!

Cryptozoology IS THE STUDY OF LEGENDARY ANIMALS, such as the Loch Ness Monster, Bigfoot . . . and the yeti.

SKIPS IS IMMORTAL.

He is also the oldest employee at the Park.

EINSTEIN'S THEORY OF RELATIVITY SUGGESTS

TIME TRAVEL

MAY BE POSSIBLE.

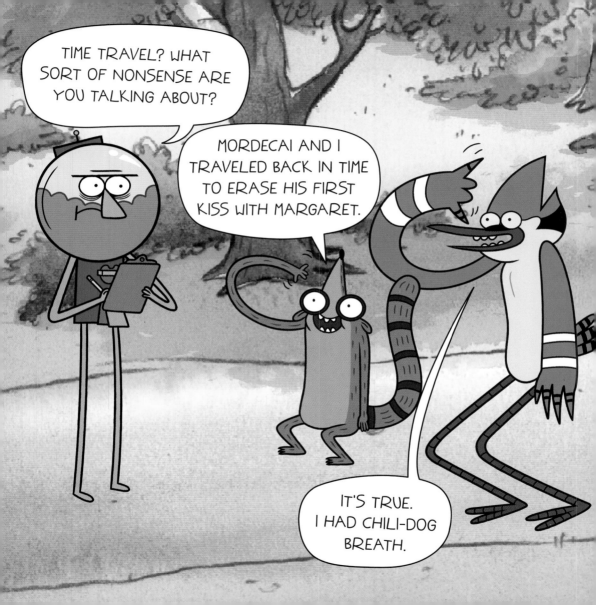

RECIPE FOR RIG-JUICE:

- 1 can of Radi-Cola
- Frozen fruit-punch concentrate
- 1 bottle of hot sauce
- Sugar Frosted Sugar Bombs
- Candy and candy wrappers
- 1 apple
- 1 can of sardines
- Pickles, pickle juice, and pickle jar
- 1 orange

Directions: Put all ingredients into a tub. Mix.

STICK HOCKEY is also known as BUBBLE HOCKEY due to the bubble-like DOME over the top.

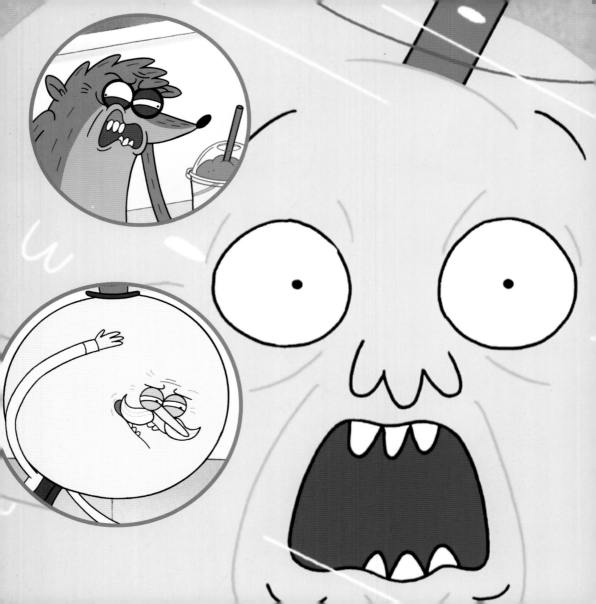

LAKE MONSTERS
LOVE PIZZA PARTIES.

Back in the '70s, everything was made out of shag carpeting.

ABRAHAM LINCOLN

USED TO STORE NOTES, LETTERS, AND BILLS IN HIS

STOVEPIPE HAT.

MR.
MAELLARD
OWNS THE
PARK,

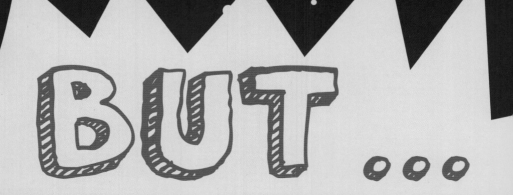

BUT
...

SKIPS IS VOICED BY MARK HAMILL. HAMILL IS ALSO KNOWN FOR HIS ROLE AS LUKE SKYWALKER IN THE STAR WARS MOVIES.

HAMILL ALSO VOICES BENSON'S DAD, ONE OF THE BABY DUCKS, HI-FIVE'S DAD, ONE OF THE UNICORNS, AND A BUNCH OF MONSTERS.

POPS CAN PLAY THE KEYBOARD, THE VIOLIN, AND THE HARPSICHORD.

The spinet, virginal, ottavino, and clavicytherium are all smaller versions of the harpsichord.

PARK EMPLOYEES

POPS

MUSCLE MAN

SKIPS

MORDECAI

HI-FIVE GHOST

THOMAS

RIGBY

BENSON

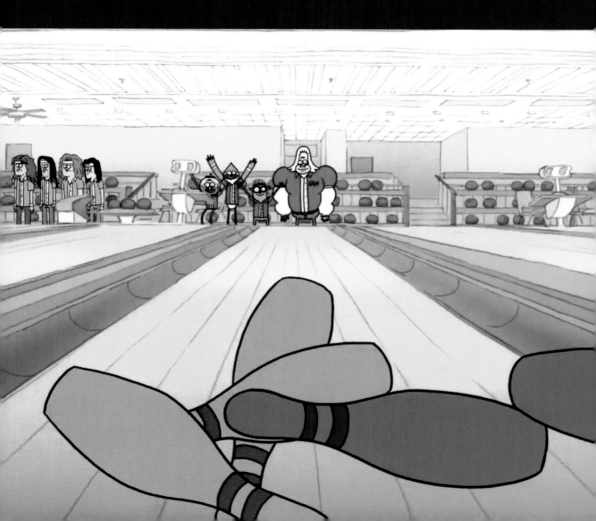

DIFFERENT VARIATIONS OF BOWLING INCLUDE TENPINS, NINEPINS, CANDLEPINS, DUCKPINS, AND FIVEPINS

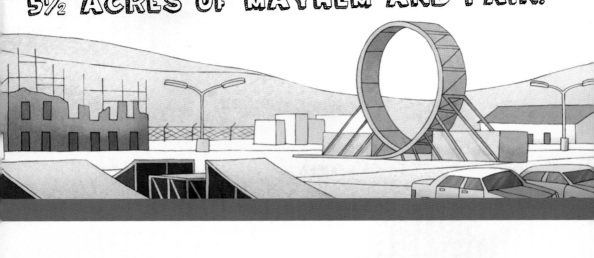

THE STUNTMAN'S FINAL EXAM IS 5½ ACRES OF MAYHEM AND PAIN.

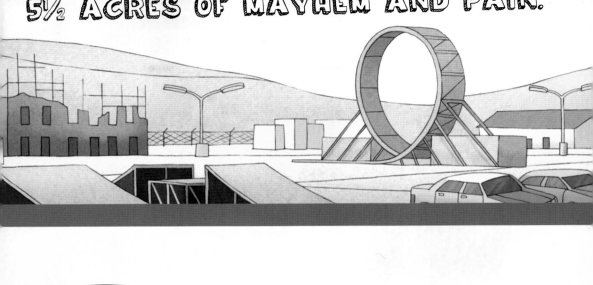

THE STUNTMAN'S FINAL EXAM IS 5½ ACRES OF MAYHEM AND PAIN.

NEVER TREAD ON A SACRED ANIMAL BURIAL GROUND.

It is believed **KISSING** originated in India. Breath mints were not invented until much later.

The study of kissing is called **PHILEMATOLOGY.**

OTHER WAYS TO SAY
Naked

NUDE

IN THE BUFF

DISROBED

AU NATUREL

IN YOUR BIRTHDAY SUIT

BARE

WITHOUT A STITCH

DIVESTED

THE FIRST FEATURE FILM WITH SYNCHRONIZED SOUND WAS CALLED *THE JAZZ SINGER*. IT OPENED IN OCTOBER 1927.

DIFFERENT WAYS TO SAY 'GREAT PARTY!'

AWESOME CHUGFEST!

Capital soiree.

WICKED FEAST!

GREAT PARTY . . .
OH, I WAS SUPPOSED TO
THINK OF A DIFFERENT ONE?

WE THROW AWAY MORE THAN 60 MILLION PLASTIC BOTTLES EACH DAY.

Be sure to use a bottle with reusable plastics to be good to the environment.

OR BETTER YET, USE A GLASS!

THE BICYCLE KICK OF DEATH WILL DEFEAT A DOUBLE DEATH SANDWICH.
The Bicycle Kick of Death

THE DOUBLE DEATH SANDWICH
is the only way to defeat the Master of
DEATH KWON DO.

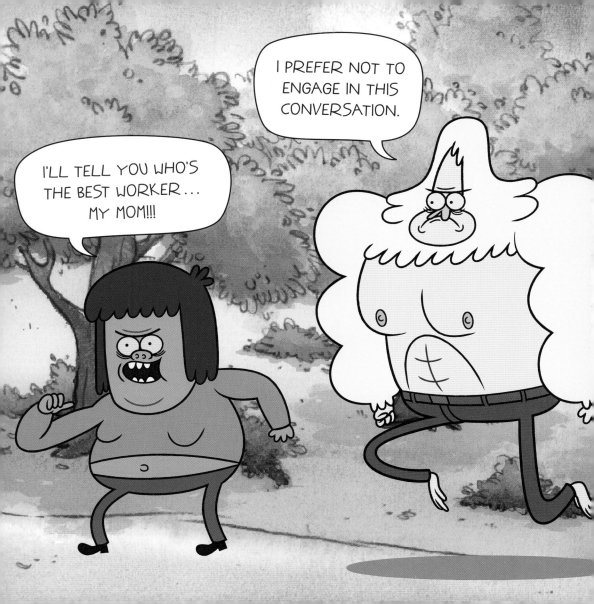